THE LIFE SENTENCE

THE LIFE SENTENCE

John 3:16

Andy Christofides

paternoster
Lifestyle

Copyright © 2002 Andy Christofides

First published in 2002
by Paternoster Lifestyle

08 07 06 05 04 03 02   7 6 5 4 3 2 1

Paternoster Lifestyle is an imprint of Paternoster Publishing
PO Box 300, Carlisle, Cumbria, CA3 0QS, UK
and Paternoster Publishing USA
Box 1047, Waynesboro, GA 30830-2047
www.paternoster-publishing.com

British Library Cataloguing in Publication Data

A catalogue record for this book is available from the British Library

ISBN 1-85078-444-2

Designed and typeset by Temple DPS Ltd, 23 New Mount St, Manchester M4 4DE

Printed in Great Britain by
Cox and Wyman, Cardiff Road, Reading, Berkshire.

1

SETTING THE SCENE

My aim in writing this book is to present the basic claims and truths of Christianity, using plain everyday words as completely free of religious jargon as I can make them.

In order to achieve this aim, I have chosen just one sentence from the Bible; perhaps it's the most famous sentence of all. Even if you have never read the Bible, it is quite likely that this sentence is familiar to you. Martin Luther, a great Christian leader of the past, said that this verse was 'the Bible in miniature' because it contains all the basic truths of Christianity. By reading, understanding and acting on this one sentence, the promise is that you can come to know 'the being who made everything' and be certain of heaven when you die – quite a sentence. It is in fact

1

the *life sentence* because it tells you how you may come to have *eternal* life.

Often at various international sporting events, advertising hoardings around the ground and banners in the crowd give the book, chapter and verse where this sentence may be found. Here it is.

For God so loved the world that he gave his one and only Son, that whoever believes in him will not perish but will have eternal life.

This sentence is found in the Gospel of John, a biography of the life of Jesus Christ written by one of his followers. You can read it in its setting in John 3:16. All I wish to do in this short book is to simply explain this remarkable statement.

Immediately, it puts people into one of two groups. As you read this page now, you are either in one or the other. Any group of people could be divided in many ways — for example by sporting interests, for some prefer soccer, some squash, some rugby, others tennis or athletics. We could divide as to which political party we support, or over our nationalities or hobbies. But as God looks at you (and everybody else) he sees you as being in one of two groups. Right now you are either *perishing* or you have *eternal life*.

To perish means simply that we do not know God here and now. Although we may know much *about* him, we do not know him. But that is not all for, unless we know God now, when we die we shall still perish, for we will be forever away from the good presence of God. (We will look at this in more detail later.)

To have eternal life means to know God here and now and not simply to know about him, but to know him. There is a great deal of difference between the two, and it is the very heart of what Christianity is all about. Christianity is not simply a matter of going to church, saying prayers, singing hymns, reading the Bible and doing good things, you can do all that and still be perishing.

Christianity in essence is all about knowing God. Everlasting life is to know God here and now, as Jesus says in John 17:3.

Eternal life begins in this life. Christianity is not 'Pie in the sky when you die.' Someone once described it as, 'Have it on your plate while you wait.' It begins here and now. We have, if you like, a taster, but its fullness is to be found in the reality of heaven.

Which group are you in right now? If you feel you are among those who are perishing, then please read this very carefully, because as you read it, if you understand it and act on it, you can transfer from the group that is perishing to the one that has everlasting life. And if you already have eternal life, the good news is that there are no transfers back.

Well, with that as an introduction, let us begin to go through this great sentence.

2

FOR GOD...

The sentence begins with these words — 'For God...' This is the best place to start on any explanation of Christianity, because its great aim is that we might know this God. So who exactly is he? When the name God is mentioned, what do you think of? A great American preacher, A.W. Tozer once wrote, 'What comes into your mind when the Name "God" is mentioned is the most important thing about you.'[1]

A recent survey in Britain found that 80% of those questioned said that they believed in God. This seems very encouraging until the next question was asked, 'And what is God like?' The answers were very diverse indeed.

To most, God was some old guy up in the sky somewhere with white hair and a long white beard. Maybe he once started the universe off, but he is now very distant and has no particular interest in us. To others, he was some kind of a force that fills the universe – rather like 'The Force' in the *Star Wars* films. Another person gave the answer that God is a brick, an ordinary red house brick!

Different religions have differing views as to who God is. To some there is only one God. To others there are many gods. To yet others, again as in *Star Wars*, 'God' is just a force. But what about the God of the Bible? Who is he? What is he like? If I am to get to know him, I must understand something of who he is.

We are often told today that it doesn't really matter what you believe as long as you are sincere. Therefore, the thought is that it's OK to have loads of different ideas about God and nobody is wrong – everybody is right.

A moment's clear thinking shows how silly such an idea is. If God really does exist, he is exactly who and what he is; there is one set of real truths about him. As you read this book, you really do exist and there are certain truths about you. You are exactly who and what you are. How crazy to think it normal that there is no ultimate truth about you. There is and your passport, for example, records some of these absolute realities. It's the same with God.

It seems that in almost every other area of life we accept the existence of truth. But when it comes to this vital area of God, we throw our brains out of the window and imagine that sincerity is all we need.

Imagine the dangers of seeing a doctor who didn't believe in absolute truth but all that matters is sincerity. You visit him in his surgery and this is how the conversation goes.

'Doctor, I have these very bad headaches.'

'OK, don't worry, take a tablet.'

'Which one?'

'Oh, it doesn't matter which one, as long as you are sincere in wanting to get rid of the pain.'

Now, would you stay with such a doctor? Of course you wouldn't because his relativism, his denial that there are 'true truths', would put your life in danger.

Some don't go so far as this. They accept that God exists and that it may be some things are true of him. But they argue that we simple little beings do not and cannot ever know these. God is so vast and so remote it is impossible to know for sure anything much about him. So, for this reason too sincerity is all that matters.

This could theoretically have been so, but for the fact that the God who does exist has chosen to let us know what he is like. He has done this in three main ways — in the nature of the material universe, in the contents of the Bible, and supremely in the amazing being of Jesus Christ.

Here, briefly, are a few of the essential things we need to understand about God, things he has allowed us to know because he has chosen to make them known to us.

GOD IS ETERNAL AND SELF-EXISTENT

The first book of the Bible — Genesis — begins with this great statement, 'In the beginning God...' Before this world came into being God was there. God is eternal, he had no beginning, and he will have no end. Go back trillions of years and God is there and he will be no younger than he is now. Go ahead trillions of years and there is God, and he will be no older. That God will never have an end, we feel able to understand. We can grasp that things go on and on, because we ourselves have awareness that we have a soul that will never ever end. But to think that God had no beginning — this we cannot understand. This is outside our experience because we had a beginning and all we experience had a start. However, God is not like us. He always has been, always will be. He simply is. This is the only answer to the often asked question, 'Who made God?' Such a question belongs to time but since God is outside time, the question is not valid.

It would be wrong, however, to think of God's eternity as being like a line consisting of past, present and future, for God is outside time. Time is something we travel through, but God does not. What is the date today? To you and me today has a definite date, yesterday is past and tomorrow is future. But what is the date to God? Well, it is all dates at the same time! God is past, present and future all at once. Right now, he is watching you being born, he is seeing you starting school, getting married, starting your first job and taking your last breath. God's eternity means that he stands outside time, unrestricted by it and sees the whole of time in one glimpse. What a God!

GOD IS THE CREATOR

'In the beginning, God created the heavens and the earth.' It is not the purpose of this book to get into a discussion on creation versus evolution, just to state clearly the claim of the Bible that God is the originator of all we see and know — and of all we don't see or know! The universe is truly awesome.

The question is often asked, 'How do you know God exists?' I believe that the very existence of the universe is a powerful argument for God's existence. Let us consider some facts.

We live on a planet called Earth that orbits around a star called the sun at a distance of some 93 million miles. Our sun belongs to a galaxy called the Milky Way which contains about 100,000 million other stars (I'm not too sure who counted them). Our galaxy is not alone in the universe but is just one of 100,000 million other galaxies. And God made all this — out of nothing — by simply speaking! That vast display in the heavens cries out to us each night, 'There is a God!'

I remember being the speaker at a boys' outdoor camp in the area around St Davids in west Wales. The nights were cloudless and moonless, and since there were no streetlights to interfere with the view of the heavens the sight of the stars was truly magnificent! I remember telling the boys at a morning meeting that if only they could have seen the sky the previous night it would have gone some way to helping them believe in God. The next night while on late night patrol, we saw lots of heads popping out of the tents viewing the glorious sight. It was great to hear their gasps of amazement. 'The heavens declare the glory of God' (Ps. 19:1).

GOD IS ALL-POWERFUL

Since God is the creator of all this, it is obvious that he is extremely powerful. The Bible declares he is all-powerful and that there is nothing that he cannot do except to do wrong. Again, just to consider the vastness of creation, the numbers I have just mentioned can leave us without a true grasp of the mind-boggling scale of things, so here's a little illustration to help.

Let's imagine you got into a fast car and wanted to travel to the sun on the newly opened interstellar highway. Let us imagine it is a very fast car and that you travel at 150 miles per hour and that you never stop for fuel, food or rest. At 150 miles per hour, 24 hours a day, 365 days a year, it would take you 70 years to reach the sun! Having been there a while, you decide to head off for the next nearest star, Alpha Centauri, some four light years away. You travel at the same speed of 150 miles per hour and 15 million years later you are approaching the outskirts of Alpha Centauri! And God made all this and beyond – he is truly all-powerful.

This is the God of the Bible! Sadly many people consider Christianity to be boring. Boring! That surely is a mindless comment. How could knowing *this* God be boring? This is the most remarkable thing that could ever be – to know this God. Let me challenge you reader, what have you got that could begin to compare with this? Your sport? Your job? Your house? The latest soap opera?

GOD IS EVERYWHERE

Wherever you are right now as you are reading this, you are where you are and nowhere else. Perhaps earlier on in the day you were somewhere else, and if so you were not where you are right now. This is a limitation that we all have. We can only be in one place at a time. God, however, has no such limitation. He is in all places at the same time. He is where you are *now*; he is where you were *now*.

There is nowhere where God is not present for he fills the Earth and the whole universe. Man has walked on the moon, God was there waiting. We are making attempts to get a manned space flight to Mars, God is there waiting.

When it is said that God is everywhere, we must not think that God is simply very big and that as we travel around we encounter different parts of him. But rather we should understand that all places contain all of God. So as you sit reading this now, it is not that a part of God is with you and a different part with me, but *all* of God is with you and with me.

GOD KNOWS EVERYTHING

There are many things that we find puzzling in life, many mysteries that we cannot solve. For example, where is Lord Lucan? In the 1970s he mysteriously disappeared following the death of his children's nanny. Nobody has seen or heard anything from him since. And whatever did happen to Shergar, the famous Irish racehorse that went missing? Who did shoot President Kennedy? These things may puzzle us, but they are not puzzles to God. He knows exactly where Lord Lucan is, and he knows exactly what happened to Shergar, he knows who fired the shot that killed President Kennedy. God knows everything.

We spend a great deal of our time in learning things. At school and college we study hard to gain more knowledge and to be taught new things. But do you know, God has never learned anything, no one has ever taught him anything, he never will learn anything! All the knowledge in all the books throughout the world, he knows. Every fact of geography, science, maths and history, he knows. He even knows the mistakes that are in books on these subjects and the mistakes that teachers make for they remain ignorant on certain things and speculate on others — but God's knowledge is perfect and complete.

Have you ever had a surprise? Perhaps you come home to find that your aunt Bessie has arrived unexpectedly and as you step in the door you exclaim, 'What a surprise!' God is never surprised.

God has total knowledge of all facts, he could sit all your exams and receive A*s and 100% in all subjects. Although this is truly amazing, God's knowledge goes much further than this. As we look at each other we see each other's faces, and although we communicate by talking and listening, we don't really know what other people are thinking. But God does. We can hide nothing from him. He knows what you are thinking right now. In fact he knows every thought you have ever had and will ever have. He knows our hopes, our wishes and our disappointments. He knows us totally. We cannot hide from him nor can we ever deceive him. God knows *everything*.

GOD IS SELF-SUFFICIENT

To have needs is a purely human thing. God needs nothing and nobody. He is entirely content and fulfilled within himself. For billions and trillions of eons before there ever was anything God existed and lacked nothing. We, by contrast, have great needs and unless many of them are met, we die.

It is said that the average human being can live for about three weeks without food; some more, some less, depending on your size! Without water, however, we would last only three days; while if our oxygen supply were cut off, death is about three minutes away. We are very fragile creatures with lots and lots of needs.

God has no needs at all. God certainly does not need you or me. I have been left feeling nauseated as I've heard Christian preachers give the impression that God needed people to believe in him. The pathetic plea goes up to a crowd of hearers, 'Oh, please, please turn to God he really does need you, look at all the trouble he has gone to, please do not disappoint him.'

God does not need us. To think that he does is entirely wrong. But we desperately need him.

GOD IS PERFECT

There are many more things that could be said about who God is and some will be mentioned later in this book, but I want to finish this chapter by mentioning one more thing. If I am ever to come to know this God it is vital that I understand this last point – that God is perfect, pure, clean, beautiful and good. The Bible calls all this his holiness. Everything about God, every aspect, every thought, word or deed is absolutely perfect.

We cannot really understand this because we know nothing remotely like it. Even the very best that we do know is blemished and imperfect. So to try to get across to us something of his perfection, the Bible uses word-pictures to illustrate the point to us. The most common is *fire*. 'God', the Bible tells us is, 'a consuming fire' (Heb. 12:29).

If we wish to purify an item to ensure it is free from all germs, bugs and microbes, the surest way is to plunge it into a fire. There are bugs that will survive disinfectants and even those that will survive boiling water, but *nothing* will survive raw fire. So to illustrate to us the great truth of God's purity and the fact that nothing or no one impure will ever survive in his immediate presence, the Bible uses the picture of fire. Now it is essential that we understand this.

Add all these truths together — that God is eternal, all-powerful, everywhere, knows everything and is perfect — and you begin to understand how packed with meaning the little word 'God' is. It is *this* God that so loved the world.

1. Tozer, A.W., *The Knowledge of the Holy* (Carlisle: STL, 1994) p.11

3

SO LOVED *THE* WORLD

The sentence continues, 'For God so loved the world...' What does God mean by 'the world'? Well, certainly this includes the physical world of rocks and trees and plants. God is concerned for the environment because it is his world, he made it. But here the word 'world' refers to people, you and me, the six thousand million living, breathing human beings alive right now. God loves people.

So who are we? There are, and always have been, two major views on this question. The first is by far the most popular in western society today. It bombards us day after day, if not directly then certainly indirectly. If people do not actually express this view of who they are in words, then they certainly express it in their actions.

Simply put, the view is this — there really is no God; we are simply the product of an event called the 'Big Bang' followed by evolution.

The Big Bang theory states that 15,000 million years ago, the universe was infinitely small and infinitely hot.[2] All that we now see and know was at that time packed into that dot which was so small it could not be seen. Where that dot came from cannot be explained. Then, for reasons unknown, this dot exploded to throw out this present universe. What a mind-boggling beginning! According to this theory all we now know was at one time packed into this microscopic point. Can this kind of beginning be contemplated?

Suppose you were set the task of crushing a snooker ball into a point small enough to pass through the eye of a sewing needle. Hopeless, don't you think! Then add the snooker table. Then the snooker hall. Then the town, the country, and Planet Earth! And on and on... Impossible, you say, yet this is what many believe existed at the beginning.

Around 10,000 million years later, our sun began to burn, Planet Earth condensed and formed and began to cool, oceans filled ... life began ... and we humans evolved.

That, *briefly* stated, is the current popular way of thinking about how the world came to be. No God, Big Bang, evolution.

Well, if this is true, we have to face up to a certain conclusion. You and I are meaningless, insignificant accidents. You cannot reasonably ask the question, 'What is the meaning of life?' because there isn't one — it is all an accident. If there is no God and Big Bang and evolution are true, then the chair you are sitting on right now would have more meaning than you because at least someone made it for a purpose, which it is fulfilling, but you would be just an accident.

As this view is increasingly believed, and as any sense of a real personal God decreases in our land, then why are we surprised that young people behave as they do? Teach them they are meaningless accidents and they will live in line with that teaching. The link is obvious. If we teach ultimate meaninglessness, people will believe ultimate meaninglessness and will live to get what they can while they can.

Right across the board as governments publish figures, there are increases in crimes of every kind; theft, burglary, rape, violence, rioting, murder ... should we be surprised? In the area of social problems we clearly see recorded increases in drunkenness, drug abuse, child abuse, marriage breakdown, divorce, gambling addictions ... should we be surprised? And what about the increasing levels of selfishness, greed and envy?

Why is there a seemingly callous disregard for the life of the unborn child? Isn't this connected with the common idea that a child is not a person until it is born? Why the constant pressure for the legalization of voluntary euthanasia and even calls for forced euthanasia? Surely we cannot be surprised at these awful realities. Tell a human being he has no meaning and these things will follow.

Here is another deeply saddening fact. The top cause of death among male teenagers, excluding accidents, is suicide.[3] This is very much on the increase.

Tell a teenager all is meaningless, and he tries to make meaning. To do this, he needs money. For many this just isn't coming through the jobs they have, so some turn to crime to add to their income. Most try to struggle along but because TV, film, video, magazines show what money can bring the despair increases.

The ache for relationships with real meaning is constant. Must have a partner, must have a best buddy. But when these fail to come, or break down, then there is often despair. To some, death seems a very reasonable option. Surprised?

But the proportion of suicides doesn't seem to be any less among the rich and the famous. How can this be? They have it all — money, possessions, relationships, fame, adulation, so what's the problem? Well, they have it all, but they discover that this *all* is in reality unfulfilling, and that is very scary!

The comedian Tony Hancock took his own life leaving a note saying, 'This is completely rational ... there was nothing left to do. Things seemed to go too wrong too many times.'[4]

He had the fame, fortune, possessions, adulation, but not the happiness he desired. And how many more come rapidly to mind from the areas of film, TV, pop and rock, who have taken this terrible step?

If it is simply Big Bang and evolution, then life is meaningless and we must face the consequences of such a bleak outlook.

This view also leaves us feeling so very small and insignificant. Right now there are 6,000 million people on this planet and you are one of that vast number. Even should you rise to some position of great fame on Planet Earth, so what? On a universal scale you remain a total nothing.

During a brief break from discussing major national and international affairs, a former president of the United States wandered onto the balcony of the White House with his secretary of state. As they looked up at the sky, the president pointed out the vastness of it all, some distant faint point in the sky in reality was a whole galaxy containing billions of stars. He spoke of the great distances, light taking millions of years to reach us from there. At the conclusion, feeling suitably humbled, they returned to their meeting.

You see, if there is no God, you really are a nothing in the vastness of it all. We all have a name, but who knows your name? Ring up your bank, building society, gas or electricity supplier, council tax office and all you are to these people and to so many more is a number. 'Account number please' is what you are asked for.

In response to this, many look to make their individual mark. The punk rock era of the 1970s was an attempt by young people to get themselves noticed above the crowd by their dress, body piercing, hairstyles and language. Toyah Wilcox sang, 'I want to be free, I want to be me.' This was a cry for the right to be an individual. It echoed the theme of so many punk songs of the era, a cry to be heard, known, seen, acknowledged.

All this is again the unsurprising result of no God, Big Bang and evolution.

But, there is a God.

And this one fact changes everything.

This God, the God so briefly described in the last chapter, made you. You are not a meaningless accident.

As a deliberate action on his part, in the misty distance of eternity past, he actually as it were sat down and planned to make you. Now, this being so changes everything. Immediately you are raised from the despairing level of a meaningless accident to a position of great meaning and immense dignity. The God behind everything made you. God does nothing without good reason, and so you can be sure there is also a clear purpose to your existence.

What is the reason for our being here? There must be more to life than the endless routine of daily living; get up, have a wash, have breakfast, get dressed, go to work or school, have lunch, work or school again, come home, have dinner, watch TV, go to bed, sleep, get up. What is it all about? Is this all there is to life?

Since there is a God, we can now rightly ask the question, 'What is the purpose of life?' And thankfully he has given us the answer. It is this: we were made to know God, to enjoy God and to bring honour to God.

Our number one purpose in life is to know personally the God who made us and who made the whole universe. What a staggering thought this is. When we think about all that men and women are doing on Planet Earth right now, what is there to compare with this? If it is possible to know God, then there is nothing with which we can compare it. There is nothing that comes close to being its equal.

Some of us may have the privilege of knowing someone famous and we perhaps like to slip into conversation that we know personally a famous sports star, TV personality or a film star. But to know God personally is way above and beyond this. It is the ultimate. It is life.

Well now, this brings an obvious question. 'If there is a God, and he made me to know him personally, then why don't I?' What's the problem?

Let's start by making it clear what the problem is not.

The problem is not our intelligence; some imagine that we do not know God because we simply are not clever enough. In 1969 we put a man on the moon, which was pretty clever, and we have advanced greatly since then. But many think that as yet we are not clever enough to know God, if indeed he is there. The problem, they say, is a matter of our lack of sufficient intelligence. Well, that is not the problem.

Others say the problem is that we don't try hard enough. We need to make more effort. The answer they believe is in religion.

A good definition of religion would be 'mankind's efforts to reach God'. Looking at the history of religion it is amazing just how hard people have tried to know God. Some have given up their lives to serve others, others have gone into monasteries, given away possessions, travelled vast distances, and punished themselves mercilessly. But God remains silent. The problem is not that we don't try hard enough.

In his useless effort to reach God, Simon Stylites (?390–459) spent over 30 years on a platform at the top of a 20 metre wooden pole. Food was sent up to him but there he stayed. He ascended the pole in 423 and there he stayed until his death. He simply cut himself off from society in an effort to reach the God he was sure existed. But it didn't work. He was clearly 'barking up the wrong pole'. However, he did impress many of his contemporaries who, copying him, became known as 'Stylites' or 'Pillar Saints'.

A more recent example would be the sincere efforts of the former Beatle George

Harrison. Before his death in November 2001, he repeated a statement he often used, 'All things can be ignored, but the search for God cannot be ignored.'[5]

The lyrics of his hit song 'My Sweet Lord' suggest that the search had not ended.

So what is the problem? It is not intellectual, it is not lack of effort – the problem is a moral one.

The Bible calls this sin.

What exactly is sin? In thinking about what God is like, the final point made was that God is perfect. Sin is to be less than God's moral perfection. Many think that sin is 'doing things wrong'. In a way that is true, but the heart of sin is not so much doing wrong but *being* wrong.

The problem all began in mankind not long after God had made the first man and woman. You can find the story in Genesis (the first book of the Bible) chapter 3. God made Adam and Eve and placed them in a perfect setting, a place of great beauty and plenty, the Garden of Eden. Although it was very beautiful and supplied all their needs, the most amazing thing about the place is that God himself was there. Adam and Eve knew God personally for he walked with them in the cool of the evening.

Now, it seems that God set Adam a kind of test. He laid the facts out before him.

'Look Adam, I made you; I am your life giver and sustainer. Stay with me, stay close, and you will live. But Adam, I have made you free. You have freedom of choice and you can choose to leave me and go your own way. But let me warn you, if you do exercise your independence and go your own way — *you will die.*'

The sad fact is, Adam and Eve chose to go their own way and suffered the awesome results, results that were passed onto his children and his children's children — to every human being including me the writer and you the reader. So sin at the heart is a matter of conscious independence from God, going our own way, living our own lives, doing our own thing.

While writing this, Timothy McVeigh, who was responsible for the bombing at Oklahoma City, has been executed in America. In his last written statement, he quoted from a poem by W.E.Henley (1849-1903).

It matters not how straight the gate,
How charged with punishments the scroll,
I am the master of my fate:
I am the captain of my soul.

Here then is the root and heart of sin – self, independence from God. Conveniently, in the English language, the middle letter of sin is the personal pronoun 'I'. Who is the most important person? Well, it is every individual person on Planet Earth, in his or her opinion.

Let me illustrate the power and reality of this problem we all have.

Imagine you have just had a group photograph taken for some special occasion. The film goes off for developing and eventually arrives back in the post. You open the packet and take out the photo. Who do you look for?

'Did he get my right side? Was my hair OK? Did that spot show up?' you might ask.

This simple illustration shows the problem we have. The heart of sin is self, I, me, mine.

Every newborn child is born with this disease of self-centredness. Nobody escapes it. A sleeping baby may look so very innocent, but just wait till he wakes! That child will demand attention and will soon learn how to have mum and dad running around.

I was recently watching three, three-year olds wanting to play with the same toy. Impossible!

'It's my turn! She's had a go! Let me have it now.'

Children need to be taught to do the right things, sharing does not come naturally to them.

Sadly this selfish, self-centred attitude is not left behind in childhood, but follows us through our lives. The outcome of this 'self' attitude is that we cannot possibly keep the beautiful law God has given to us. (You can find this law recorded in Exodus chapter 20). In summary, God's law simply says, 'Love God with all your strength and love your neighbour as yourself.' It is a truly wonderful law, but we cannot keep it, for *we love ourselves too much!*

Take for example the seventh commandment, which demands sexual faithfulness. A man makes a promise to a woman to be faithful and to stay with her 'till death us do part'. A few years go by, children come along, and then he leaves for another woman. Why?

'I don't love her anymore, I want this new woman, I love (lust would be a better word) her instead, I need her, I can't help it.'

And what about the children?

'Oh, they'll get over it, they'll come to understand.'

And so the man leaves a distraught wife and distressed children. Why? Because *self* is all that really counts.

Let's look at the tenth commandment. The demand here is that we should be satisfied with what we have and not be constantly desiring that which others have. The commandment could be re-worded, 'You shall not keep up with the Jones's.'

But all the time we in the western world want more and more. Year in year out we see our economies growing. What happens to the growth? Well, we consume it on ourselves. Have you ever wondered why millions starve to death (really, they do!) while we continue in relative luxury? Well, they starve and die because we want more and more.

Do you know that we as a nation give less than 0.5% of our annual national income in foreign aid? There is a way to take a big step towards ending world poverty by upping that 0.5% to a more realistic 10%! Does that sound good? Suppose a political party came along with such a policy, but to implement it they explain they would need to put 10% on the basic rate of income tax. I wonder how many votes they would get. Meanwhile the millions continue to starve.

The outworking of this soul disease is appalling, and we could go on and on with more and more illustrations to drive home the point. But the attitude is, 'So what? I'm doing OK. So what if I'm a sinner, I'm enjoying myself.'

This is very true, sin is enjoyable, even very enjoyable, otherwise people wouldn't sin! However, sin brings consequences. The sentence we are looking at mentions the word 'perish'. The result of sin is that we perish. Another sentence in the Bible puts it like this; 'The wages of sin is death' (Romans 6:23). The term 'wages' here is very interesting. A wage is something we deserve, something we have earned. You work hard all week and at the end, you have earned your wage. God is telling us here, that we have worked hard at sin all our lives, and so we have earned our wage... *death*.

This 'death' has three aspects to it.

Firstly, it is a spiritual death. Sin cuts us off from God; it puts a barrier between us (Is. 59:2). This explains why you are not even sure whether or not God exists, and if he does, you have no real idea what he is like.

Sin has brought spiritual death.

This explains why there are atheists. Cut off from God because of sin, they stand on a tiny speck called Planet Earth, in a tiny speck of a solar system, in a tiny speck of a galaxy in the vastness of the universe, and arrogantly say, 'God does not exist.' How can they know?

This spiritual death is a great tragedy and it is the reason for the lack of fulfilment so many feel. In each of us there is a hole that no thing or no one can fill; it is a God-shaped blank that only he can fill.

This is a theme much sung about in modern pop music. Here are a few examples. The Rolling Stones sang about not being able to get any satisfaction.

The 1980s group The Police sang about there being a hole in their lives.

The band U2 declared that despite all their efforts, they still hadn't found what they were looking for.

Despite their great success and fame, the God-shaped blank remains and so these Pop stars sing of their experience, an experience we can all identify with.

Here then is the first death, spiritual death, because we are separated from God. But the response of many to this is, 'so what, I can manage without him'.

While holding a weekly Bible study aimed at those inquiring about the Christian faith, a lady interrupted with a very interesting question.

'Excuse me,' she said, 'I don't wish to be rude, but I have a good husband, three lovely children, my husband and I both work, we have a lovely home and are all very happy. Why do I need your God?'

This sentiment was firmly expressed by many callers to Nicky Campbell's *Radio 5 Live* phone in. Mr Campbell was interviewing Luis Palau, an Argentinean evangelist. Mr Palau in explaining the Christian faith said, 'Do you know Nicky, there is no real life outside of knowing God.'

Well, the phone lines went mad with indignant callers correcting Mr Palau by stating how very happy they were with their godless lives.

My reply to the lady and Mr Palau's replies to the callers were much the same. First, you may be 'happy' now, but what are you comparing this to? What is your point of reference? The 'life' that is found in knowing God is of an order way above anything this world can offer, and you have to experience this to know the difference.

But, perhaps more importantly, what happens when the 'good times' end and difficulties arrive? The job is lost, the home is repossessed, the child dies, the husband leaves...?

Still more importantly, sin not only brings spiritual death, it brings that great enemy and most unwanted intruder, physical death. And what an intruder it is, how unfair it so often seems!

Do you know, we were never meant to die. If sin had not infected us we never would have died. That is why it seems so unfair, particularly when a close friend or a family member dies, it seems so out of place. 'Why has this happened to me?' is the cry of our hearts.

But die we must. From the moment we are born, the process of decay and death starts its work in us. As you look at a fellow human being all you can see is death. The outer layer of skin is already dead and flaking away. As you read this book right now, I know almost nothing about you, but one thing I do know is this — you will die one day. It is an appointment you must keep. It may be sudden, you may get lots of warning, but you will die.

Think about those lovely sleek, black limousines that wind their way through our towns, going from house to house and then on to the cemetery. They eventually call at every house, including yours. Are you ready for this?

In the cemetery of my hometown in Lancashire there is an epitaph, which I first read in my early teens. It struck me then and has remained with me since.

Remember me as you pass by,
As you are now so once was I,
As I am now so you must be,
So be prepared to follow me.

Death comes to us all. Are you prepared for this awesome event?

Many do bravely face death without God. A prominent atheist facing death recently was asked if his thoughts had turned to God. 'Oh, I haven't fallen for that old potato' was his reply. Very brave, but is he wise?

The final consequence of sin is the third aspect of death, which we must now look at. Physical death is not the end. Deep down we seem to feel that there must be something else. What happens when we die? The epitaph I have quoted read 'be prepared to follow me'. Where to? This epitaph is actually found in many graveyards and I am told that under one someone has chalked,

To follow you I'm not content
Until I know which way you went!

So, which way do we go?

You and I are body and soul. It is the soul that thinks, decides, plans, debates, likes, dislikes, communicates, creates and ponders the future. Animals do not have a soul. Your dog or cat is not sat down right now planning his summer holiday. While you may create a picture of your dog, he will not do one of you. Your dog does not think of death, God and eternity. Such things are uniquely human; they are concerns of the soul. At the point of death, the soul, the real you, leaves the body and is launched into forever. You come to an encounter with God. We are all believers at this point!

If at the time of death, we still have this soul disease of sin, we carry it with us for eternity. God will give us the final judgment, your final wages — separation from him forever, punished by him forever, to die forever in a real place the Bible calls hell. This is the final aspect of God's punishment of sin, eternal death. This is what it means to perish.

Some may still bravely say, 'Well, if hell is

separation from God, good. I didn't want him on earth and I don't want him in eternity!' This may sound brave, but it is very foolish. The separation received is a separation from his goodness. Here and now on Planet Earth, whether we know God or not, he is being good to us. He provides food, air, water, shelter, human companionship and a sense of well-being. But there, in eternity, hell is God's goodness withdrawn, and we are left with what the Bible calls his wrath. For all eternity, sinners are the objects of God's wrath. The exact nature of this wrath is impossible to describe. God does not 'fly off the handle' in a rage. His wrath is his 'settled opposition against sin'. Whatever words I could use here would fail to do justice to the awful horror of hell. It is enough to say avoid it at all costs. Here is the ultimate end of sin, so avoid it!

But how? The next amazing part of this life sentence introduces us to the source of escape!

2 Hawking, S.W., *A Brief History of Time* (London: Bantam Press, 1988) p.117

3 HMSO, *National Statistics – Mortality Rates,* General 1999 (London: The Stationery Office, 2001) DH1, No.32

4 Joffe, E., *Hancock's Last Stand* (Lewes: The Book Guild, 1998) p.133

5 *Daily Mail,* 1 December 2001

4

So *Loved* the World

I remember hearing a sermon given by a famous old Welsh preacher in my student days in Cardiff. I vividly remember him leaning over the pulpit, pausing, looking around at us all and saying in a most gentle voice, 'If you remember nothing else of all I have to say, don't forget this...God loves you.'

As it happens, many years later, I have forgotten all he said, the text, passage, all the words he spoke, apart from those most stunning words.

And they really are stunning! The problem is we have heard them said too lightly too often. It has become a pat phrase that has lost any real meaning. Let me attempt now to put some meaning back.

One of the most basic needs we have is

the need to be loved, liked, cared for, and wanted. To have the genuine love of a fellow human being is a tremendous thing. Sin has made such a mess of things that it is often said that a dog is a man's best friend! There is a sad amount of truth in this. Man, made to know and love God, made to love his neighbour as himself, finds his best friendship is with his pet. And this is the case for many, especially the elderly. The only person they talk to, the only one who listens, is their pet.

But way above any pet, way above any fellow human being is this Supreme Being, the eternal, the first cause of all things; and he loves you.

Writing as a scientist, I very much appreciate the science of logic, and one of the most thrilling things I have found in the Christian message is the sheer logic of it all — with the exception of this statement that God *loves* us. It actually makes no sense, for if you probe and ask why God loves us the only answer that comes back is because he does.

So, I must admit, here we have a problem that cannot be solved as to why God loves us. But it is a problem I am most content to be stuck with.

However, words are so easy. How can I know that God loves me?

Yes, words are easy, and here is a great part of our problem. So often we can hear the words 'I love you' when what the person means is 'I lust for you; I desire what I can get from you; I want to use you to help me.'

Jill and I got married in 1980, we now have four lovely children, and although I am not good with words I still love her and always will. Occasionally, not often enough, but occasionally I will tell her I love her. But I am sure that for Jill, as for us all, actions speak far louder than words.

Imagine now that I kept on saying to Jill, 'I love you,' but kept her locked up in an iron cage. Each day I fed her a few crusts and a glass of water, but continually said, 'I love you.' Wouldn't she have every right to say 'No you don't!' My words are saying

'I love you,' but my actions are denying it. Love is more than words. Words are easy.

In the mid 1990s I was flicking through the TV channels and came across a famous pop artist singing his latest offering at an awards ceremony. The song finished, and the audience went ridiculously wild in their applause. The singer then received his award and floated up to the lectern to make his thank-you speech. I have forgotten all that he said that night apart from this. 'I want you all to know...' looking around at his audience, then giving a sickly stare into the camera, head rocking from side to side like a noddy dog... 'I want you all to know that I love you, I love you all so much.' The old Welsh preacher's words have never left me, and these words have also stuck fast in my memory. The old Welsh preacher's words lift my heart, the words of the singer turned my stomach. He didn't love me! How could he love me? He didn't even know me. And what had he ever given me apart from a headache?

You see, words are easy. The words 'I love you' are used so often in a glib and deceitful way that they lose any real meaning. But when God says he loves us, he doesn't just say it; he proves it in his actions. God has powerfully demonstrated his love for us. He has demonstrated his love in such a way that it is beyond any doubt that he does love us. It is an act of such love that in trillions of years from now it will not be forgotten. Let's have a look at the next part of the sentence.

5

HE GAVE HIS ONE AND ONLY SON

We have now come to the main part of this sentence, God's Son. He is known as Jesus Christ. Jesus is his given name, Christ is his title. He is not the son of Mr and Mrs Christ who had a child and called him Jesus. Christ is his title. Christ is the Greek word for the Hebrew Messiah, which means the anointed or the promised one.

The Old Testament of the Bible is full of promises about the Messiah (Christ), one who would come to 'save' his people. These promises detail every area of his life and death. Here are just a few examples. If you have a Bible you could take some time to look them up.

The place of his birth is mentioned (Mich. 5:2), and the tribe he would come from (Gen. 49:10). We learn that he would be a descendant of King David (2 Sam. 7:11-13; Ps. 132:11-12 — the immediate reference here is to David's son Solomon, but there is clearly a reference to an eternal ruler, see Jer. 23:5-6). We are given details of the Messiah's three-year mission (Is. 35:5-6; 61:1-20), of his death and the nature and meaning of it (Ps. 22:1,6-8,14-18; Is. 53). We are told of his rising from the dead (Ps. 16:9-10). And, be assured there are many, many more prophecies of the Messiah's coming and mission. If this area were of interest to you, then perhaps Josh MacDowell's *New Evidence That Demands A Verdict*[6] would be a good book for you to read.

Looking at the great detail of the prophecies about 'the Christ', all of which were fulfilled in Jesus in exact detail, it can really be said that his biography was written and finished four hundred years before his birth. Imagine going to a publisher today with the manuscript of a biography of a man to be born in the twenty-fifth century!

Jesus Christ was born around 4BC in Palestine. He lived to the age of thirty-three at which point he was executed. For three years from the age of thirty, he toured his native land saying and doing the most staggering things — things that so enraged the religious authorities that they plotted to get the Roman authorities to execute him. There is no doubt that he is a historical figure, for a number of contemporary historians wrote about him.[7,8] The question is not 'did he exist?' but 'who was he and what did he do?'

WHO IS HE?

Let's look at the first question, 'Who is he?' Now here is a question that has raged for two thousand years. Doubts as to who Jesus is are not new. As he went about his work, public opinion was widely divided. Some said he was a prophet, others thought him a great teacher and yet others a liar and deceiver. Some thought that he was mad or even possessed by the devil. Even his own disciples remained unsure about him after two years following him around. So, reader, if you too are not sure, join the long list of others who have not been sure.

A while ago I came across a piece of writing by Napoleon Bonaparte. In it he is giving his conclusions as to who Jesus is. While he does not reach the right answer, I greatly admire the fact that he had at least carefully read the Gospel accounts of the life of Jesus Christ and so he had earned the right to express an opinion. Here are his thoughts.

'I know men; and I tell you that Jesus Christ is not a man. Superficial minds see a resemblance between Christ and the founders of empires, and the gods of other religions. That resemblance does not exist. There is between Christianity and whatever other religion the distance of infinity... Everything in Christ astonishes me. His spirit overawes me, and his will confounds me.

Between him and whoever else in the world, there is no possible term of comparison; he is truly a being by himself. His ideas and sentiments, the truth which he announces, his manner of convincing, are not explained whither by human organization or by the nature of things ... the nearer I approach, the more carefully I examine, everything is above me – everything remains grand, of a grandeur which overpowers. His religion is a revelation from an intelligence which certainly is not that of man ... One can absolutely find nowhere, but in him alone, the imitation or example of his life ... I search in vain in history to find the similar to Jesus Christ, or anything which approaches the gospel. Neither history, nor humanity, nor the ages, nor nature offer me anything with which I am able to compare it or explain it. Here everything is extraordinary.'[9]

Now, while Napoleon is to be admired for at least considering Jesus Christ and studying the life accounts, his opinion was still not right, for Jesus was a man, but so very much more than a man. So who is Jesus Christ?

Our sentence calls him God's Son. The name often given to him in the New Testament is the Son of God. But what does this term mean?

First, we must be absolutely clear what it does *not* mean. It does not mean that 2,000 yeas ago, God suddenly had a son through a woman called Mary. Many believe, including most Muslims I have met, that this is what Son of God means. Such a thing is as grotesque and horrifying to Christians, as it would be to any Muslim!

Neither does it mean that at some point back in eternity, God acquired a son and then sent him to earth on a mission. What then *does* it mean?

The account of the life of Jesus Christ written by the disciple John, starts with a breathtaking account of Jesus 'in the beginning'. In this account, he calls Jesus 'the Word', that this is Jesus is clear from verse 14 of the first chapter. Here are those opening lines.

'In the beginning was the Word, and the Word was with God, and the Word was God. He was with God in the beginning. Through him all things were made; without him nothing was made that has been made.'

'In the beginning.' When was that? Well, forget time here; it was before time, in the depths of eternity. Go back as far as you can or wish and eons beyond eons of eons into forever past and way beyond and you will always find that Jesus was 'with God'. This tells us that he is eternal; he has no beginning, for in the beginning, Jesus was with God.

So far, so good. But this next bit is mind blowing!

'...and the Word *was God*.'

Now, what do you make of that? Jesus was not only with God, having a distinct identity from God the Father, but he was God. Here we have facing us a part of the mysterious truth of the trinity. God is one, yet God is three Persons. Not three Gods; one God, yet three Persons. And if you find your mind can't quite take that in, good! We are dealing with the being of God, and while there never will be anything about him that is unreasonable, there will be parts that are *above* our reason! That is an important distinction.

Even in the area of physical science, there are seeming contradictions that on the surface are baffling. Take light for example. Experiments can be done to show that light travels as a series of particles, packets of light or photons. Experiments also show clearly that light travels as a waveform. Now light cannot be both and yet it is both. Baffling? This is certainly above the reason of most humans and is known as the 'duality of light'. But there are some 'egg heads' who are actually able to resolve this apparent conflict, and maybe you are one of them!

Back to our main point, Jesus is God the Son; John goes on to emphasize this by saying he created everything that there is.

Around the time 4BC, when Caesar Augustus reigned from Rome, God the Father so loved the world, that he sent God the Son

(Jesus) into the womb of a woman called Mary who lived in a tiny part of the world called Palestine. Mary was firmly engaged to a man called Joseph, but the child to be born was not the son of Joseph. He was the son of Mary, but also the Son of God. How did this happen? In his account of the life of Jesus, Luke tells us, 'The Holy Spirit came upon her and the power of the Most High overshadowed her' (Lk. 1:35).

This then involved the work of the third Person of the trinity. God the Father sent God the Son under the agency of God the Holy Spirit.

The child was born in Bethlehem as prophesied and placed in a cattle-feeding trough in the barn of an inn.

Now who is he? Stay with this, because there are a few more things I must mention.

In eternity, he is fully God, God the Son, creator of the universe, creator of you and me. He is in eternity with the Father and the Holy Spirit. But, he left there and he was born of Mary. Mary's egg, mysteriously fused with the divine, produced... who?

The God man.

Wow!

Do you know I love *Star Trek*; I am a real 'Trekky' fan. My favourite series is *The Next Generation* with Captain Jean-Luc Picard. What amazing adventures he and his crew have, exploring strange new worlds, seeking out new life forms and new civilizations ... boldly going where no man has gone before! Mind blowing, but not true; sadly it's all made up.

But this ... this is far beyond what anyone could make up, and it is *true*, and we've only just begun! Jesus Christ is the God man. He is fully God and fully man. He is not half and half, neither is he some mixture of the two. He is and functions as, *fully* God and *fully* man.

This is clearly seen in his life on earth; at times he acts as only God can, yet at others he shows his humanity.

On one occasion, Jesus and his disciples were in a boat out on the Sea of Galilee. A violent storm blew up and the disciples were convinced that they were going to die. They woke Jesus who was, amazingly, asleep at the back of the boat, and said to him, 'Don't you care if we drown?' Jesus stood up and commanded the storm to stop, which it did immediately. His shocked disciples said to each other, 'Who is this? Even the wind and the waves obey him?' (See Mk. 4:35-41.)

Now this is divinity. Many times I'd have loved to say 'Rain, rain go away, come again another day' and for it to work. But it never has! Such power belongs to God alone.

On another occasion, a friend of Jesus called Lazarus died. Jesus arrived on the scene four days after his death. Jesus went to the tomb straight away and said, 'Roll away the stone.' 'But Lord,' they protested, 'there will be a stink, he's been dead four days.' But at Jesus' insistence they did as he asked. Then came the command, 'Lazarus (and Jesus had to be specific!) come out!' He came out, alive and well (see Jn. 11: 38-44).

Yet, there were times when he clearly showed his full humanity. After a long day in the hot sun, he really was thirsty. After a hard day of teaching and healing, he really was tired. After a period without food, he really was hungry. In no way can we say that tiredness, thirst or hunger belongs to God. These are purely human experiences, and Jesus has them. He is the God *man*.

Not surprisingly, the Old Testament got this one right too. Isaiah tells us that the Christ will be Emmanuel, which means 'God with us' (Is. 7:14).

The next question to any thinking person has to be this. 'But why would God, the great God we looked at in chapter 2, come to this tiny, tiny speck, and become a tiny, tiny speck on a tiny, tiny speck?'

WHY DID JESUS COME?

From our sentence we see that Jesus' mission has a double aim – to stop us from perishing, and to give us everlasting life. His mission is very much included in his name.

The name Jesus means, 'God is salvation' or 'God saves'. Before the birth of Jesus, an angel appeared to Joseph in a dream and said, 'You shall call his name Jesus because *he will save his people from their sins.*'

Now, in this section, let's look at this explanation of the name Jesus, 'he will save his people from their sins'.

First of all, what does 'save' mean? It's a word we use quite a lot. In this case it means to rescue someone from great danger when there is no way they could have helped themselves.

Please don't get the idea that I'm a TV addict! But another kind of programme I enjoy watching is the emergency rescue type, where people get into all kinds of amazing difficulties and are wonderfully saved.

Imagine the scene. Mr Jones was out walking one evening along a remote cliff top, when suddenly he lost his footing and fell over the edge. Luckily, he managed to grab hold of a tree root sticking out of the cliff face and was able to hang on about 20 feet down the cliff face. But who would see him there? Night was drawing in, and the root was slowly giving way.

Meanwhile, Mr Smith was taking his dog for a walk. He wouldn't normally have gone along the cliff path, but his dog had seen and chased a rabbit for some distance and Mr Smith had to follow. Suddenly, Mr Smith heard a faint cry for help. He looked over the edge of the cliff and there was Mr Jones some 20 feet below, hanging on for dear life. There was no way Mr Smith could reach him, and the root could have given way at any moment. What could be done? He had no time to go to the town for help. Amazingly, right there on the cliff top path was a mobile phone that Mr Roberts had dropped that very morning. Mr Smith picked it up, called the emergency services that rushed to the scene and rescued Mr Jones.

Well, what a story! Now what had happened to Mr Jones? He had been *saved*. He was rescued from great danger when there was no way he could have helped himself. He was about to be dashed to pieces on the sharp rocks beneath. But someone came from the outside and rescued him.

This is exactly what Jesus does. He is the one who rescues us from great danger when there is no way we can help ourselves. He saves us, not from being dashed on rocks, or drowning, or from a fire, but from a far more serious situation. He came to save us from sin and its terrible consequences.

In previous chapters we have looked at what sin is and at what it does. Maybe you felt, as many do, that the bit about hell was outrageous. On hearing of hell and what it's like, people often react by saying things like, 'Oh, God is a God of love, and he would never send anyone to hell.' Or expressed more aggressively someone will say, 'Oh, I'd never believe in a God who could do something so awful as to send people to hell. If that's God, I don't want to know him, thank you very much!'

Well, as much as God is a God of love, he

is also a God of justice, and the ultimate penalty for sin is hell. But he is a God of love, and to stop you from going to hell, he went there himself in the person of Jesus Christ.

This was his mission, and he fully accomplished it; to pay sin's penalty for us, to take the wages we have earned and to buy us a place in heaven. And what a price he paid!

So far, I have said that the Gospels (Matthew, Mark, Luke and John) are accounts of the life of Jesus Christ. In a way that is true, but on looking closer, you see something very odd. The main theme is not his life, but his death. Far from being life stories, a more accurate description would be 'death stories'.

Take John's account; of the 21 chapters that make up his book, 11 focus on his last week, and 10 on his last 18 hours. Very strange indeed!

Usually a biography is all about a person's life; background, birth, childhood, life's work and achievements. I recently read a biography of that incredible military genius,

Alexander the Great. Of the 250 pages of the Penguin Classics edition,[10] only one paragraph is given to the event of his death. This is very understandable. The interest in Alexander is in his truly great achievements in his life. His death was an unexpected tragedy.

But the focus of the Gospels is on the death of Jesus Christ, because this was *his* greatest achievement. This is why he came. He was born to die. We want to live; he came to die.

As we saw in the last chapter, the death of the Messiah was prophesied in the Old Testament, hundreds of years before Jesus was born. Far from being a surprise to him, Jesus often spoke of his death and tried to prepare his followers for this event (Mk. 8:31-32; 10:32-34).

Jesus knew he would die, when he would die, where he would die and how he would die. He tells his followers that he is in full control of his death; *he* is setting the agenda and the timetable. This is what he said. 'The reason my Father loves me is that I lay down my life — only to take it up again. No one takes it from me, but I lay it down of my own accord. I have authority to lay it down and authority to take it up again' (Jn. 10:17,18).

Even at his execution, Jesus is still in full control. He dies when he is ready, not before, not later. His final words were, 'It is finished' (Jn. 19:30). To which John adds the telling comment, 'With that, *he* bowed his head ... and *gave up* his spirit'.

Not only was he in full control of every aspect of his death, most importantly, he knew *why* he would die. It was no sudden tragedy, but an event planned to the smallest detail in eternity and with a definite purpose in mind — to save sinners from hell.

You see, sin will have its consequences, full payment is due from every sinner and the ultimate horror of that price was outlined in chapter 3 — hell, and that forever. How could a God of love send anyone to such a place?

Well, here at this point the love of God is expressed in its full glory, because to stop us from going there, he went there himself in the person of his own Son. We all die as a result of our own sins, but Jesus Christ had none for he lived a perfect life. So why is he dying, and dying such a death? Let's hear the reason from his own lips. 'For even the Son of Man did not come to be served, but to serve, and to give his life as a ransom for many' (Mk. 10:45).

Jesus Christ died to pay a price, the price you and I would and should be paying now and for eternity. The penalty for sin is death, spiritual, physical and eternal. We deserve that death, but Jesus paid it for us. What a price; what a death!

6 McDowell, J., *New Evidence That Demands A Verdict* (Carlisle: Alpha, 2000)

7 Tacitus, *Annals of Imperial Rome* (London: Penguin, 1989) p.364

8 Pliny, *The Letters of Pliny The Younger* (London: Penguin, 1969) p.294

9 Cunningham, R., *Discovering Christianity* (Leicester: UCCF, 1992)

10 Quintus Curtius Rufus, *The History of Alexander* (London: Penguin, 1988)

6

THE CROSS

Crucifixion is perhaps the most terrible form of execution ever devised by mankind. Its aim was of course to kill, but to do so by inflicting the maximum pain on its victim, and for as long a time as possible. Some victims would linger between life and death for a number of days. The aim was also to expose the victim to maximum indignity and humiliation.

The victim was laid naked on a wooden cross to which he was then firmly secured by nails hammered through his wrists and his feet. The cross was then hauled upright and the poor wretch left to die naked, exposed to the full glare of the elements (the scorching of the Middle Eastern sun and the cold chill of its nights), and the gaze of the mocking bystanders.

Such was the experience of Jesus Christ. Prior to his crucifixion, he had been stripped, savagely whipped, beaten and a crown made of long eastern thorn briars rammed on his head. This is the God of creation, the Lord of glory being crucified. At any point he could have stopped this obscene treatment and obliterated his tormentors with a mere thought. Why does he allow it? He loves you, and his desire is that you should be in heaven – so he goes through with it.

Gathered round the cross, his enemies are full of glee. They mock him mercilessly, saying, 'He saved others, but he can't save himself! Let this Christ, this King of Israel, come down from the cross, that we may see and believe' (Mk. 15:31-32).

He was fully able to do this... and *what* a temptation! But he didn't, because he wants *you* in heaven. Sin did this to Jesus Christ. But in reality, he has only just begun to pay our penalty, for much worse was to come.

Mark, in his account, tells us that after Jesus had been on the cross for three hours, suddenly, at midday, the sun was blotted out and darkness covered the land until three in the afternoon. During this time Jesus cried out into the darkness, 'My God, my God, why have you forsaken me?'(Mk. 15:34).

What is happening? Well, for three hours, man had done his worst to Jesus Christ; now, God the Father takes over and for the next three hours he will pour out his righteous anger against sinners upon his own Son. During this second period, the cross of Jesus Christ set up on a hill called Calvary, outside the city of Jerusalem became 'hell on earth' as the Father poured out on his Son the punishment we deserve.

Isaiah, the Old Testament prophet saw this event seven hundred years before it happened. Here are his words. 'But he was pierced for our transgressions, he was crushed for our iniquities; the punishment that brought us peace was upon him, and by his wounds we are healed. We all like sheep have gone astray, each of us has turned to his own way; and the Lord has laid on him the iniquity of us all' (Is. 53:5-6). These verses explain exactly what is happening to Jesus Christ in those second three hours. He is taking upon himself the hell that we deserve. What was it like? We will never know! Even if we were to end up there, we will still never really know what Jesus went through since we would be there of our own sin – he was there for a vast number of sinners. One poem puts it this way.

We may not know, we cannot tell,
What pains he had to bear,
But we believe it was for us
He hung and suffered there.

At three o'clock he dies. He has accomplished his mission. He has 'given his life as a ransom for many'.

Now here is a most interesting question. 'How can those few hours on the cross pay for my *eternity* in hell?' Well, the answer is to an extent part of the mysterious area of Christianity, but surely it is all tied up with the

Person on the cross. Jesus Christ, remember, is *fully* man and *fully* God. Because he is a man, he is able to pay mankind's penalty — *man* has sinned so *man* must die. And on the cross, man did die! But since he is also fully God, then we have on the cross the infinite and the eternal one, and in the plan of God, those three hours pay an infinite and an eternal price.

Here, then, is the meaning and the purpose of the death of Jesus Christ on the cross. It is all put so well in the poem from which I have just quoted; here it is in full.

There is a green hill far away,
Outside a city wall,
Where the dear Lord was crucified
Who died to save us all.

We may not know, we cannot tell,
What pains he had to bear,
But we believe it was for us
He hung and suffered there.

He died that we might be forgiven,
He died to make us good;
That we might go at last to heaven,
Saved by his precious blood.

There was no other good enough
To pay the price of sin,
He only could unlock the gate
Of heaven, and let us in.

O, dearly, dearly has he loved,
And we must love him too,
And trust in his redeeming blood
And try his works to do.

Cecil Frances Alexander (1818-95)

WHAT NEXT?

As we have seen, Jesus not only spoke of his death, but also of his resurrection. The real, physical resurrection of Jesus Christ is an essential part of the Christian faith because it tells us two vital things. First, he was who he said he was. Many people can claim many things. A number of years ago a famous sports commentator, David Icke, made the claim that he was the Son of God as he went around dressed in a turquoise shell suit. He later retracted the claim and put it down to a time of confusion.

If I made the claim to be 'Superman', the only way to prove the claim would be to fly around for a while, send laser beams from my eyes and do a quick change in a phone box. I may get somewhere close to the third, but the first two things I cannot do. I am not Superman.

When Jesus claimed to be the Son of God, his enemies challenged him to prove it. The only proof he promised to give was his resurrection from the dead (Jn. 2:18-22; Mt. 12:38-40). On the third day, he rose, as he promised – he *is* the Son of God.

Secondly, the resurrection of Jesus Christ proves that his death in our place was effective and that our sins can be forgiven.

From a logical point of view, it can be said that his resurrection was inevitable. Since he had done nothing wrong, how could death keep him?

In illustrating this point, Derek Swann, an old preacher friend of mine, used this striking illustration of Death receiving Jesus Christ after the crucifixion.

'Now when Jesus breathed his last on Calvary, Death took him into custody (as it does all of us). You can imagine Death calling for the book of Jesus' life to be brought in for inspection. Page after page would be turned but not one sin would be found anywhere. Only the last page remains and when that is turned, like the others, it is spotless. Death turns pale and, motioning to those around, says, "Let him go, his life is sinless, we have no grounds for holding him." The resurrection was inevitable.'[11]

Is this enough?

We have seen that Jesus Christ came to die our death, and that his resurrection proves his death was effective as a payment for our sin, but is that enough to get us to God and heaven? Surprising as it will seem to some, the answer is no, it is *not* enough! It is a tremendous thing that Jesus should die as a penalty for my sin but, to know God and to get to heaven, I need something more than my sins paid for. I need a perfect life.

The good news is that Jesus lived this for me too. This is a vital fact often left out in presenting the Christian message. The life of Jesus Christ is as vital to you and I as his death. The life Jesus lived here on Planet Earth for 33 years was absolutely perfect. He never sinned, for he kept the law of God completely, in thought, word and deed.

His enemies, though they tried very hard, could find nothing wrong with him. On one occasion he challenged a crowd, 'Can any of you prove me guilty of sin?' (Jn. 8:46).

Nobody could. We know today how effective the press can be at exposing the errors of the famous, yet in the case of Jesus, his enemies could find nothing at all with which to accuse him.

His friends could find no faults either. Now, perhaps we can fool our enemies, but it is very difficult to hide our faults from those nearest and dearest to us. If I were to meet a group of people for the first time and slip into our initial conversations, 'Oh, by the way, I am perfect', perhaps for a while I could carry it off. If one of the group were then to ask my wife about this matter, the truth would soon come out!

But, in the case of Jesus, his closest friends believed him to be absolutely pure (1 Pet. 2:22; 1 Jn. 3:5).

At the trial of Jesus Christ, the only charge brought against him by the religious authorities was that of blasphemy for claiming to be God, and for this they wanted him crucified. The callous but weak Roman governor who had to give the final order to execute Jesus states several times, 'I find no fault in him' (Jn. 19:4,6). But he still hands him over to die.

All these opinions and statements are stunning, but the only opinion that really counts is that of God the Father. What did he think of the life of his Son Jesus Christ? Well, we need not wonder, because on two separate occasions, he spoke these words from heaven, 'This is my Son, whom I love; with him I am well pleased' (Mt. 3:17; 17:5).

There it is, the *vital* opinion of God!

The final witness to the perfect life of Jesus is of course, the resurrection. Had Jesus been a sinner, Mr Death would have kept him in the tomb.

Jesus lived a perfect life, he fully kept the ten commandments of God, and he did it for us. That life was essential to us getting to heaven. In a very real way, Jesus sat the entrance exam for heaven in our place. The pass mark is 100% perfection and Jesus passed, only he could.

There was no other good enough
To pay the price of sin,
He only could unlock the gate
Of heaven and let us in.

11 Swann, D., *Evangelical Magazine of Wales* (Bryntirrion: April/May
   2000) p.6

7

So, Now What?

So far in this 'life sentence' we have been looking at history, and the things that God has done. But this was all 2,000 years ago. If the death of Jesus Christ on the cross has really dealt with the problem of sin, why is it I still don't know him?

Well, there is one part of the sentence yet to be looked at, and it deals with you and your response to the things you have read. Miss it out, and you die. You personally will take the full force of God's punishment. You personally will know something of what Jesus took on the cross. You will continue to perish now, and for all of eternity.

But, take this step and you personally will come to know God here and now, and be guaranteed heaven when you die.

So, what is this step? Now it is just here

that so many people go so very sadly wrong. They feel that the thing to do now is either to reform yourself, or to get religious. Both steps are fatally mistaken.

What does the sentence say?

'For God so loved the world that he gave his one and only Son, that whoever is a nice person shall not perish but have eternal life.'

Thankfully, it doesn't say that. It is not how good you are that counts. It is not helping other people, buying a poppy, doing meals on wheels.

Well how about this?

'For God so loved the world that he gave his one and only Son, that whoever gets religious will not perish but have eternal life.'

Thankfully again, it does not say this. It is not your prayers, church attendance, Bible reading, baptism, christening, confessions, ceremonies, holy communions or any other religious observance you can add that gets you to God. In fact, add them all together, do them all frequently and you will still perish without this one and only vital step. Here it is. 'For God so loved the world that he gave his one and only Son, that whoever *believes* in him shall not perish but have eternal life.'

You must believe, simply and exclusively believe. Believe that you are a wrath-deserving sinner. Believe that Jesus Christ is the God man. Believe that he lived, died and rose again for you.

When you believe a great legal exchange takes place. The sin of your life as a whole, from the moment of your birth to the point of your death, and the principle of sin you were born with, *all* your sin, is placed to Jesus Christ's account when he paid for your sin on the cross. The pure perfect life he lived is then put to your account and God now views you as he views his Son – perfect!

The barrier of sin having gone, we come to know God now and are sure of heaven when we die. What an amazing sentence is this 'life sentence'. Let me urge you, reader, to make sure you have believed. If you are still unsure and want to know more then here are a few things you must do.

PRAY. Prayer is talking to God. Be honest with him, tell him you would like to believe, tell him your doubts and ask him to help you.

READ THE BIBLE. Get a good clear translation (the New International Version or New King James are helpful) and read the life of Jesus in Matthew, Mark, Luke and John.

ATTEND A GOOD CHURCH. It is vital that you hear this message being preached. To do this you must go to a church where the minister believes the Bible to be the truth, the whole truth and nothing but the truth. Don't be shocked, but not all do! You will get a good clue from the church notice board. Do they have a prayer meeting? Is there a midweek Bible study? If you attend on a Sunday, is the bulk of the time given to the preaching? If the minister really believes the Bible is God's word, it should have been.

A final point. Some people have problems with being sure that they have believed and received eternal life.

How can you know you believe?

Well, there is an inevitable fruit that comes along with belief. True belief brings with it *repentance*. Simply put, this means a sorrow for sin, and a real and radical change of life. While I was perishing, I lived for me. If I have eternal life, I now live for him. Oh I still fail; God counts Christians as being perfect because of Jesus, but in reality we remain sinners – saved sinners. But deep down, I now *want* to please God. He comes first.

This deep-down change is the new life that God has put in us. When we believed, there was more than a legal exchange taking place in the accounts of heaven, there was a real change in us and it will show.

A good test as to whether or not we have eternal life is to have a good look at ourselves. How is my life and who am I living for?

Put bluntly, if I live as if I am perishing (for self) then it is very likely I am perishing.

But if I live as if I have life (for God) it is very likely I have life. And if I have life then I will grow in my knowledge of God, not only here in time but also in eternity.